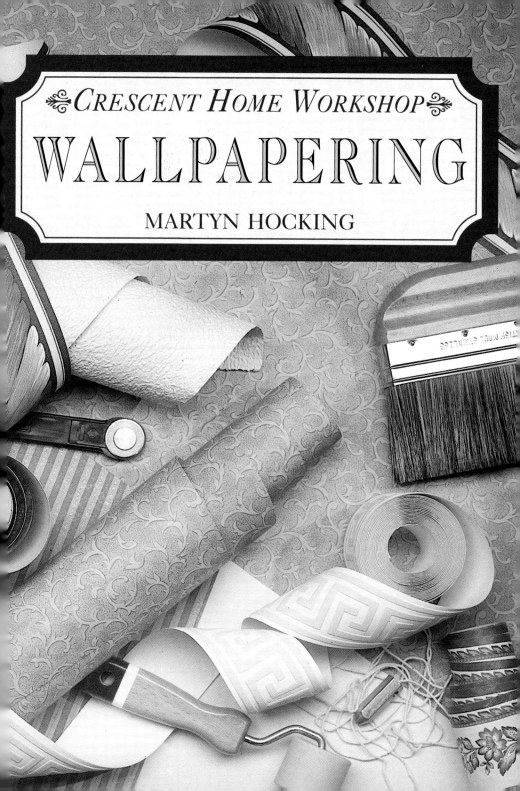

CRESCENT HOME WORKSHOP

WALLPAPERING

MARTYN HOCKING

CRESCENT HOME WORKSHOP
WALLPAPERING

MARTYN HOCKING

CRESCENT BOOKS

NEW YORK • AVENEL, NEW JERSEY

Page 2: Cool blues painted on a relief wallcovering give this bathroom a clean fresh look.
See page 8.

This 1994 edition published by Crescent Books,

distributed by Outlet Book Company, Inc.,

a Random House Company,

40 Engelhard Avenue, Avenel, New Jersey 07001

RANDOM HOUSE   New York • Toronto • London • Sydney • Auckland

Copyright © 1994   Harlaxton Publishing Limited

Copyright Design © 1994   Harlaxton Publishing Limited

2 Avenue Road, Grantham, Lincolnshire, NG31 6TA, United Kingdom.

A member of the Weldon International Group of Companies.

Publisher: Robin Burgess

Design and Coordination: Rachel Rush

Editing: Martyn Hocking

UPS Translations UK

Illustrator: Jane Pickering

Photography: Chris Allen, Forum Advertising Limited

Typesetting: Seller's, Grantham

Color Reproduction: GA Graphics, Stamford

Printing: Imago, Singapore

Title: Crescent Home Workshop - WALLPAPERING

ISBN: 0-517-08781-2

INTRODUCTION   7

CHOOSING WALLCOVERING
    COLORS AND PATTERNS   8
    WHICH WALLPAPER TO USE?   9
    WHICH ADHESIVE TO USE?   14
    HOW MUCH PAPER WILL I NEED?   14

GETTING STARTED
    WALLPAPERING TOOLS   16
    PREPARING THE WALLS FOR PAPERING   19
    WHERE TO START   21
    HANGING PAPER ON PLAIN WALLS   22
    MIXING PASTE   22
    MEASURING AND CUTTING   26
    PASTING PAPER   28
    HANGING THE FIRST LENGTH   29
    TACKLING CORNERS   30

SOLVING COMMON PROBLEMS
    PAPERING AROUND A DOORWAY   33
    PAPERING AROUND A WINDOW   34
    PAPERING AROUND A FIREPLACE   36
    PAPERING AROUND A LIGHTSWITCH   38
    PAPERING BEHIND A RADIATOR   40
    PAPERING AN ARCHWAY   41

WORKING OVERHEAD
    PREPARING THE ROOM   44
    PREPARING THE CEILING   44
    WHERE TO START   45
    PAPERING THE CEILING   46

For as long as we have lived in houses with four walls and a roof, we have felt the need to decorate them. The medieval baron covered his walls with rich tapestries, while his poor relations used canvas or wool hangings.

In the 16th and 17th centuries, the fashion was to paint interiors using a whitewash mixed with red, blue, and green pigments, but patterned papers too began to be used to line chests and closets.

Wallpaper grew in popularity to such an extent that in Britain a special tax was imposed on its purchase by the end of the 17th century. At this time, paper was still being stretched over a wooden frame and nailed to the walls.

It was the development of machine printing in the mid-19th century that turned wallpaper into a product for the masses. At six cents a roll, sales increased from one million rolls in the mid 1830s to over 30 million rolls forty years later. By comparison, the hand-printed papers they superseded cost up to 4 dollars each – a small fortune at the time.

Today our choice of wallcoverings is regarded as a fashion statement and we re-decorate our home as often as we change our car.

This book takes you through the practicalities of the job, from bringing home the pattern books to smoothing down the last seam. It is a project anyone can tackle, promising almost instant results for very little outlay.

OPPOSITE: A beautifully coordinated wallpapered room, in relaxing shades of blue and pink.

Home Workshop
CHOOSING
WALLCOVERINGS

Finding the most suitable wallcovering can be a daunting task, given the array of patterns available to the home decorator. Here are a few simple guidelines to help you through the maze of pattern books and samples.

COLORS AND PATTERNS

Color will probably be your first consideration. All too often we opt for neutral beiges, creams, and off-whites because we are afraid of making mistakes with stronger shades. As a result we end up with uninspiring interiors.

Let the seasons be your guide here and you can choose from a bolder color palate with confidence. Warm summer shades – reds, oranges, and yellows – create a warm atmosphere that is ideal for living-rooms, dining-rooms and hallways. Winter colors – the blues and greens – create a cooler, cleaner look that suits most bathrooms and bedrooms.

Few people want to decorate an entire room in a strong primary color, of course, and this is where a color-wheel can be used to good effect.

A color-wheel is a visual device which will help you to build up complementary color schemes, in which carpet, drapes, walls, and woodwork all work together to create a harmonious effect.

A color wheel shows the three primary colors – red, blue and yellow, interspersed with the shades you create by combining them – hence, green appears between yellow and blue. As a general rule, any two colors that sit directly opposite each other on the wheel will complement each other. For example, a green carpet will work well in a room with warm red walls.

While you might choose a plain green carpet, you are unlikely to opt for plain red walls – they would simply overpower you because red is a primary color. Instead, a percentage of each color would be used – a dark green with a pinkish-red, for example.

Patterns play an important part here too. The red you choose might appear as a delicate floral pattern on a predominantly white background, for example.

Similarly, if you were going to use a combination of blue walls and a warm orange or yellow carpet, the wallcovering might be a blue-and-white pinstripe rather than a solid block of color. The more white used in the background, the bolder the shade of your chosen color you can use without it becoming overpowering.

Texture is the final ingredient you will have to consider when choosing a new look for your walls. Generally speaking, smooth textures enhance a cool, uncluttered design, while heavy surface detail works best in rooms where a warm atmosphere is required.

OPPOSITE: Summer shades of reds, oranges, and yellows, give life and warmth to this room.

WHICH WALLPAPER TO USE?

There is a remarkably broad range of wallcoverings available if you are prepared to seek them out. Some are much easier to hang than others and there are substantial price differences between the mass market designs found in large hardware stores and the more unusual papers offered by designer decoration stores.

LINING PAPER – inexpensive material used to cover slightly uneven walls and ceilings prior to hanging a decorative wallcovering. Varying thicknesses are available, but none of them will disguise a badly damaged surface – you would be better off repairing the cracks and dents with plaster and sanding the wall flush.

STANDARD WALLPAPER – consists of a single sheet of paper with a design printed on the face. Price is generally a good indication to the quality of the paper – the least expensive (and thinnest) are more prone to tearing when they are wet with paste. Standard wallpapers cannot be cleaned easily, so do not use them in the kitchen or bathroom.

WOODCHIP – consists of two layers of paper with tiny fragments of wood trapped between them. A cheap wallcovering that is invariably painted over after hanging. The chips tend to make the paper fray when trimmed, but if you are painting over the top, any ragged edges will be easy to hide.

BELOW: Examples of two different effects that the creative use of color achieve in a bedroom.

'Naomi'- Bedroom Book: Forbo-Lancaster Ltd.

'St. Tropez'- Riviera: Storeys Decor.

RELIEF WALLCOVERINGS – have a three-dimensional surface pattern and are also intended to be painted with emulsion after hanging. The variety of patterns available is huge, from the subtle and understated to the downright brassy. Some have a vinyl surface, which makes them easy to clean and particularly suitable for kitchens and bathrooms. Others, known as "blown" wallcoverings have a 3-D surface pattern that feels spongy to the touch. Relief wallcoverings are easy to handle but take care not to crush the pattern in your enthusiasm to flatten lifting seams.

HIGH RELIEF WALLCOVERINGS – deserve to be treated as a separate product group, if only because they are so much more expensive than any other type of sculpted paper.

Wallcoverings of this type are sold in stiff sheets rather than rolls and are far more durable than conventional wallcoverings. The backing paper needs to be soaked prior to pasting. They are very traditional in style and will be hard to find outside specialty stores.

FABRIC WALLCOVERINGS – are for those with a taste for the unusual. Silk, burlap, oriental grass, sisal, and suede finishes are all available if you are prepared to seek them out in specialty interior design stores. They are generally much more expensive than other papers, though, and are hard to hang without leaving very visible joints.

BELOW: A practical vinyl tile effect wallcovering adds style to the kitchen.

'Victorian Tile' - Jenny Wren: Storeys Decor.

VINYL WALLCOVERINGS – are particularly suitable for wet areas like kitchens and bathrooms where standard papers would suffer from the effects of moisture in the air. Vinyl is also particularly suitable in hot and humid parts of the country. The wallpaper can be wiped clean in seconds if food splashes over it. A PVC layer has been fixed over the paper backing material during manufacture to create this hardy hybrid, which is probably the easiest wallcovering of all to hang.

Most vinyl wallcoverings are sold ready-pasted – that is, they have a layer of dry adhesive on the back. Ready-pasted papers need to be soaked in a water-trough for a couple of minutes before they are hung in order to soften this adhesive.

FLOCK WALLCOVERINGS – have a velvet overlay bonded to them to create an impression of luxury. They are relatively expensive and too fragile for busy "work" areas of the home.

OPPOSITE: A pretty flock wallcovering has a luxurious effect on a simple room.
BELOW: A touch of class added to a room by using a high relief peel-and-stick border.

'Osborne'- Fablon Profile Prints: Forbo-CP Ltd.

WHICH ADHESIVE TO USE?

There are a number of adhesives or "pastes" that are suitable for hanging wallcoverings. Most are starch-based (the starch being derived from wheat) and are sold in powder form for mixing with cold water, though more expensive ready-mixed pastes are available.

If you are hanging lining paper or standard wallpaper, a cheap "regular" paste will do, but heavier papers like relief wallcoverings and flocks need a thicker adhesive and there are "heavy-duty" glues formulated for this purpose. If in doubt, opt for an "all-purpose" paste which can be mixed with varying amounts of water to achieve the required strength.

Vinyl wallcoverings should always be hung using a paste that contains a fungicide to prevent mold growth on the wall behind. It is essential to wash your hands after handling this type of adhesive and to keep it away from children and pets.

HOW MUCH PAPER WILL I NEED?

It is worth taking the time to make an accurate estimate of the number of rolls of wallpaper you are going to need before you start. You will more than make up this time by only needing to make one trip to the stores.

By purchasing all your wallpaper at the same time, you will also be able to ensure that all the rolls come from the same manufacturing batch. Rolls made at different times (in different batches) can vary in color quite markedly even though they carry the same design. Look for a sticker on the packaging of each roll to find the batch number.

To work out how many rolls you will need, start by measuring the dimensions of the room. Measure the height of the room from the baseboard up to the molding or – if there is no molding – to the ceiling itself. Then measure the distance around the four walls to arrive at a total for the "length" of the room. Include in your measurements all doors and windows except ones which stretch from floor to ceiling (french doors, for example). Although you will save some paper at these points, you will still need to paper the walls above and below the openings. It is far better to buy slightly too much paper than to run short.

The table on the next page will enable you to work out how many rolls of paper you will need for each room. It is based on the standard US roll size which will cover 30 square feet. If this is the first time you have hung wallpaper, it would be as well to add an extra roll to allow for cutting mistakes, tears, and creases.

The table has been calculated on the assumption that the paper does not have a pattern that you will have to match up horizontally from one length to the next. If you are working with a patterned paper, you will obviously have to waste some in the matching process, and the larger the pattern the more you will waste. Allow one extra roll per room for a paper with a small pattern, two extra rolls for one with a large pattern.

It is worth knowing that most retailers will give you a refund on any unopened rolls of wallpaper that you return to them promptly.

OPPOSITE: A classic look using vinyl wallcovering adds style and intimacy in a dining-room.

WALLPAPER CALCULATOR

HEIGHT of WALLS	LENGTH of WALLS							
	30ft	36ft	42ft	48ft	54ft	60ft	66ft	72ft
6FT 10IN THROUGH 7FT	4	5	6	7	8	9	10	11
7FT THROUGH 7FT 6IN	5	6	7	8	9	10	10	11
7FT 6IN THROUGH 8FT	5	6	7	8	9	10	11	12
8FT THROUGH 8FT 6IN	5	6	7	9	10	11	12	13
8FT 6IN THROUGH 9FT	6	7	8	9	10	11	12	13

'Cabbage Rose'- Winton Hall: Storeys Decor.

Success in wallpapering relies on patience and attention to detail rather than owning an expensive set of tools, but there are a number of essentials that nobody can really do without.

WALLPAPERING TOOLS

1: CUTTING-GUIDE – metal tool which can be used as a straight-edge when cutting paper with a trimming-knife. The paper is tucked slightly under the guide before it is cut to ensure there is no gap left between the paper and either the ceiling or baseboard.

2: LADDER – to reach the ceiling comfortably, you will need to stand on something. A ladder is more stable than a chair and offers you a platform on which to place tools.

3: PAPERHANGING BRUSH – a soft brush is needed to smooth out any folds in the paper as you hang it. This prevents creasing and tearing. It is also useful for working any air bubbles trapped behind the paper out toward the edges. The wider the brush, the quicker you can work, 8in-10in is ideal.

It is vital that the brush remains clean and dry, to avoid marking the face of the paper.

4: PASTE BRUSH – a wide-headed (5in-6in) brush with synthetic bristles is needed for applying paste to the back of the paper and/or the walls. An old paintbrush can be used for this purpose but one with natural bristles will quickly absorb water from the paste and swell up, making it a less accurate tool to work with. If you are going to use a paintbrush, make sure it is a clean one.

5: PASTE BUCKET – a plastic bucket is needed for mixing the paste. A shallow plastic bowl is not really suitable as the mixing action has to be fairly vigorous. A bucket used for other household chores can be used, but again make sure it is clean. Tie a length of string across the top of the bucket, attaching the ends to the handle. This is used to wipe excess paste off the brush as you work.

6: PASTING TABLE – the first requirement of any would-be decorator is a flat surface on which to cut and paste paper. Do not be tempted to use the dining-room table for this purpose – water and paste spills will quickly take their toll. A traditional alternative has been to take an internal door off its hinges and use this, but again, the surface will inevitably suffer.

It is well worth investing a few dollars in a folding table that is solely used for wall-papering. A pasting table will be light enough to carry around from room to room and can be calibrated along its edges for easy measuring.

Basic paste tables have a plain hardboard top which is perfectly adequate, but more sophisticated models are available with a waterproof vinyl surface which can be wiped clean more easily. The latter may have a measuring grid printed on the surface and offer other features such as clip-on paste troughs, paper-roll holders and cutting aids.

A pasting table will usually measure around 6ft x 2ft when extended.

7: PLUMB BOB – a plumb bob is an essential tool if you want to hang your paper vertically. A bob is simply a metal weight attached to a length of string and is used to make a vertical line on the wall prior to hanging your first length of paper. Few walls and ceilings are perfectly square, so you will need to use your plumb bob regularly as you work your way around the room to keep the paper edges vertical.

If the edges are not kept vertical, you will have serious problems matching up any pattern or design when you come to hang the last length of paper next to the first.

OPPOSITE: A selection of essential tools that nobody can really do without.

8: SEAM-ROLLER – this is a small plastic wheel attached to a handle that is used to smooth down edges that are lifting immediately, after the paper has been hung. Do not press too hard or the paper will be damaged.

**Never use a seam-roller on embossed or blown
vinyls which have a sculpted surface pattern.**

9: SPONGE – a clean sponge should be kept on hand to wipe any excess adhesive off the face of the paper before it has a chance to dry.

10: TRIMMING-KNIFE – a sharp knife can be handy for trimming the paper at the top and bottom once it has been positioned on the wall. Professionals use scissors here, but this requires a good eye. The blade must be sharp to prevent tearing or "chewing" of the paper.

WALLPAPER PASTER – for large-scale papering projects, it is worth considering investing in a pasting machine. These can paste lengths of paper in a fraction of the time it takes to do the job by hand and in this respect do away with the need for a pasting table. What they do not provide you with is a clean work surface on which to measure and cut paper. A paster should be regarded as an extra, rather than an essential piece of equipment.

11: WALLPAPER SCISSORS – a sharp pair of scissors with long blades (around 10in) is needed to cut the paper without tearing it. Obviously, the longer the blades the easier it is to cut the paper in a straight line. Stainless steel scissors will not rust, but it is important to clean them after each papering session to prevent paste drying and hardening on the blades.

12: WATER TROUGH – a trough that you can fill with cold water is an essential piece of equipment for hanging ready-pasted wallpapers that need to be soaked to soften the adhesive. The trough needs to be long enough to take a full width of paper without folding.

**Water troughs are usually made from plastic
and are inexpensive to buy.**

PREPARING THE WALLS FOR PAPERING

Wallpaper is just that – paper that you hang on a wall – and as such has no capacity to conceal lumps, bumps, or cracks in the surface. You will be wasting both time and money if you attempt to hang a new covering over an uneven or damaged wall without giving any thought as to how it might be repaired.

Papered Surfaces

2

In most instances, the first stage in the preparation process will be to strip off an existing wallcovering that has out-stayed its welcome.

This can be done in one of two ways:

1 The traditional way is to soften the adhesive while holding the old paper in place, using a sponge and a bowl of warm water, and then strip it off with a scraper. This is a slow and often tedious business, with the paper often coming away in tiny fragments. Adding a little dishwashing liquid to the water will help.

2 The modern alternative is to hire or buy a steam-stripper which is a hot-water kettle that feeds steam to a hand-plate. The plate is pressed to the wall and softens the adhesive in seconds, allowing you to peel off large sections of the wallcovering in one go.

Paper that has been painted with latex paint should be scored with a trimming knife to allow the water or steam to penetrate the surface.

The top layer of a vinyl wallcovering can be stripped off dry, leaving the backing paper in place. This can be left and used as a lining paper for the new wallcovering.

It is not essential to strip off the old wallcovering. If it is still firmly attached to the wall, you can simply paper over the top, provided of course that the old wallcovering does not have a raised surface design.

Painted Surfaces

Walls that have been previously painted with a water-based paint need only a wipe with strong household detergent diluted in warm water to be ready for papering. If there is any sign of the paint flaking, rub the damaged areas with coarse-grade abrasive paper first.

Walls that have been coated with a solvent-based paint will not offer your wallpaper adhesive a lot of grip, and for this reason they need to be rubbed all over with abrasive paper to roughen them slightly.

Textured paint is a different kettle of fish and should be stripped completely before you paper. Special chemical solutions are available for this purpose, but a steam stripper can also be effective.

Bare Surfaces

Plaster and drywalls need to be "sized" before they can be papered. This is done by brushing a diluted solution of wallpaper adhesive over the surface and then leaving it to dry. Sizing reduces the capacity of both surfaces to absorb moisture and makes it easier to slide lengths of paper into position once they are on the wall.

Damaged Surfaces

If you find the plaster coming off with the paper when you strip the walls, or if it uncovers ugly cracks, it is essential to have the damage repaired before proceeding further.

Small repairs can be made using filler (available both ready-mixed in tubes and tubs, and in a powder form to which water is added), but large-scale damage demands the attention of a professional plasterer. Leave any repairs to dry out thoroughly and then sand down any rough spots before sizing and papering the walls.

WHERE TO START

G iven that the joints between each length of paper and its neighbors should be invisible, where you start is relatively unimportant.

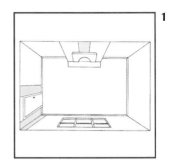

1 However, having said that, if you are hanging a wall-covering with a bold pattern, it makes sense to center it on the focal point of the room – a fireplace or the middle of the wall facing the doorway.

2 The other point to bear in mind is the distance from your intended starting point to the first pair of internal corners (external on a fireplace wall) you are going to encounter.

To avoid creasing, it is essential that you do not attempt to turn more than 1in of paper onto the adjoining wall (see page 30). This will mean trimming the paper vertically at almost every corner you tackle. While this will not be particularly noticeable if you are only cutting 2in-3in off each length, it will look ridiculous if one of the lengths is only 2in-3in wide!

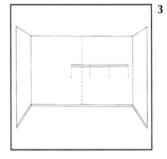

3 To guard against this, mark your intended starting-point in pencil on the wall and then use a roll of wallpaper as a measuring guide to divide up the space between this point and each of the corners. If this indicates that you are going to be forced to hang a very thin strip of paper in either corner, adjust your starting-point accordingly.

HANGING PAPER ON PLAIN WALLS

When you have prepared the surface and settled on your starting-point, your next task is to draw a vertical line through it on the wall. Use a plumb bob to find true vertical and – if you can – get a friend to help draw the line while you hold the bob.

1 It is essential that you hang the wallcovering vertically. Failure to do so will not only make accurate pattern matching impossible but will leave you with an awkward strip to cut at an angle off the last piece of paper to butt it up against the first.

2 Do not assume that the walls and ceiling of the room you are working in are perfectly square. Few are – hence the need for a plumb bob to give you a verdict.

MIXING PASTE

1 Unless you are using a ready-mixed adhesive or a ready-pasted wallcovering, you will need to mix the paste in a plastic bucket before you hang the first length. Pour the cold water in first and then add the powdered adhesive, following the manufacturer's instructions with care to achieve the right consistency. Stir the mixture with a clean wooden spoon and then let it stand while it thickens up. This will take a few minutes.

2 While the paste is thickening, clear the room to be papered of all furniture and cover the floor with newspaper or dust sheets to catch any drips or scraps of sticky paper. You are now ready to set up your pasting-table and assemble your toolkit (see page 16).

OPPOSITE: A bold pattern should be centered on a focal point in the room. See page 21.
NEXT PAGE: Painted walls need preparation before applying wallcoverings but a peel-and-stick border overcomes any preparation problems and adds an extra dimension.

'Lydiard Dining Room' - Mayfair Matchmaker-Forbo-Lancaster

MEASURING AND CUTTING

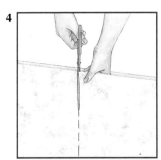

4

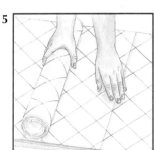

5

1 Unwrap your first roll of paper and lay it face up on your pasting table. Decide which way you want the pattern to run if you have a choice, and measure the distance between the top of the baseboard and edge of the ceiling or molding.

2 Add an extra 4in to this figure so that the paper will overlap the wall top and bottom when it is initially hung. This overlap can then be trimmed to precisely fit the baseboard and ceiling profile.

This may appear wasteful, but if you do not allow any overlap you will inevitably be left with ugly gaps where the ceiling or baseboard is uneven, and be forced to trash whole lengths of paper.

3 You may decide that you want a particular motif or portion of the design to sit just below the molding or just above the baseboard. If so, turn the wallcovering over and trim your first length accordingly.

4 Cutting should always be done with the wallcovering face downward on the pasting table. This allows you to lightly draw a cutting line in pencil across the surface for your scissors to follow. Always use a metal straight-edge (ruler) to guide your pencil. Use a pair of scissors with long-blades to make the cut.

5 If you have a pattern to match, cut several lengths of the wallcovering to size before pasting any of them onto the wall. This allows you to match the pattern "dry".

6 To do this, turn your first length of paper face up on the table and unroll a second length beside it. Align the the pattern on the two lengths and then mark the second lightly on the face to indicate where it should be cut. Then turn it over and mark and cut it to size.

7 Repeat the process with a third and fourth length and then number them on the back before commencing pasting. Before hanging Number Four, dry-match and cut another couple of lengths, and continue this process as you work your way around the room.

OPPOSITE: Remember to dry-match and cut several lengths of patterned wallcovering, as in this bedroom, before pasting and hanging to avoid problems with matching.

PASTING PAPER

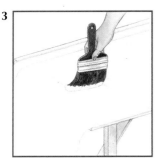

1 Lay the first length to be pasted face down on the table with the bottom end hanging down toward the floor and the top overlapping the table by about half an inch.

2 Load your brush with paste and apply the solution thickly along the center of the paper.

3 Use the brush to spread it out from here to the edges, making sure that the entire surface is pasted. If you work with your back to the light, any dry areas should be clearly visible. Take care at the end that is only just overlapping the table – this overlap is designed to stop paste getting onto the worksurface, while allowing you to coat right up to the edge of the paper.

4 When you have pasted the top half of the paper, fold the end in (paste to paste) far enough to allow the unpasted portion to lie flat on the table.

5 Paste this portion in the same way and again fold the end in toward the center. It is important not to crease the paper when folding it.

6 Carefully lift the wallcovering off the table, holding it in the center with the two loops hanging down either side. Most coverings need to be left for a few minutes while the paste soaks in, so you will need a clean, empty space on which to place them.

7 Alternatively, you can suspend them from a broom-handle that has been laid across the backs of two chairs.

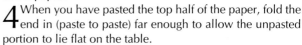

HANGING THE FIRST LENGTH

1 Pick up the first length of paper, holding it in the center to avoid creasing the two folds. Climb up to ceiling height and carefully unpeel the top fold.

2 Press the top portion of the paper onto the wall, sliding it across the surface until it is perfectly aligned with your pencil mark. The top edge should overlap the ceiling or molding by about 2in. Ease the paper off the wall and reposition it if any folds in the paper are threatening to crease.

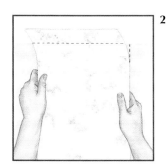

2

3 Brush out any air bubbles or folds in the top half of the paper, working from the center outward. Only when you are happy with the position of the top half of the paper should you unfold the bottom half.

4 If you have positioned the top half correctly, the bottom half should fall naturally into place, its edge butting up neatly against your pencil line. Smooth down all the edges.

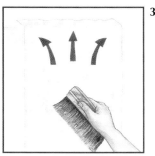

3

5 The bottom edge should overlap the baseboard by about 2in. Crease it in the angle formed by the wall and baseboard and do the same at the top of the wall.

6 Trim off any excess paper straight away – if you leave it until you have hung three or four lengths, the adhesive will have started to dry out. The quickest – and neatest – way to do this is to peel the paper back from the wall and cut along the creases with your long-bladed scissors. If you lack the confidence to do this, you can cut most wall-coverings while they are still pressed against the wall, using a sharp trimming knife.

6

7 Hang the second and third lengths in the same way, butting each up against the other. Do not allow the edges to overlap – the ridges this creates will be very obvious when the paste has dried. A seam-roller will come in handy to press down all the edges, but do not press too hard or you risk damaging the paper. Never use a roller on a wall-covering with a relief pattern.

8 Patience is important here – wet paper tears easily. An hour spent hanging the first two or three lengths is time well spent if they are hung vertically and the pattern is matched well. Improvised tools often work better than those available from stores. The tip of a rounded teaspoon handle, for example, is ideal for closing up and smoothing over joints between two lengths of paper.

TACKLING CORNERS

1

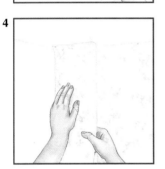

4

Few corners in a room are perfectly square – house-builders simply do not work to the same standards of accuracy as engineers. As a result, wallpaper will always start to crease and twist out of true vertical when it is wrapped around a turn.

To overcome this problem, trim your wallcovering vertically so that you are not turning more than 1in around the angle of the corner.

To avoid hanging very narrow strips of paper at the corners – which can look odd as well as being wasteful – you must plan for corners when you decide on your starting point (see page 21). Assuming that you have avoided this potential pitfall, this is how to tackle internal corners:

1 Measure the gap between the edge of the last full width of covering that you have hung and the corner. Measure this gap at several heights, as the walls may slope slightly and note the widest measurement. Add 1/2in to this figure unless the wall slopes by more than this amount, in which case you will need to turn 1in.

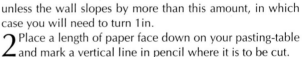

2 Place a length of paper face down on your pasting-table and mark a vertical line in pencil where it is to be cut.

3 Cut along this line using long-bladed scissors and reserve the strip of excess paper. Do not throw it away.

5

4 Paste the trimmed paper and leave it to soak in the normal way, then hang it, matching one edge to the last piece you hung, then brush the other gently into the corner.

5 If the corner is fairly square, the strip of wallcovering that you have turned around the corner should lie flat. If it has creased, make a series of horizontal cuts with your scissors at intervals along the edge to ease this problem.

6 Now measure the width of the excess paper you cut in (3) and mark a vertical line with your plumb bob this distance along the return wall. Paste and hang the excess strip on the return wall, using this line as a guide. It may be necessary to overlap the edge of the last length of paper in order to follow this line, but it is essential that you do so.

6

External corners are tackled in exactly the same way, except that you can generally turn slightly more paper around the angle without it creasing.

OPPOSITE: Dealt with one at a time, multiple corners can be a simple task.

Home Workshop
SOLVING
COMMON PROBLEMS

Papering around doorways, radiators, and air-conditioning units can seem a daunting task if you have never been shown the correct way to tackle them. But with a little knowhow, none of them should hold you up for too long.

BELOW: Doorways and other obstacles are made simple with a step-by-step approach.

'Clevedon Hallway'- Mayfair Matchmaker: Forbo-Lancaster Ltd.

PAPERING AROUND A DOORWAY

At first sight, this looks like a job that is going to involve a lot of detailed measurement in order to be able to mark and pre-cut the paper to fit around the door frame. In fact, there is no need for any of this work.

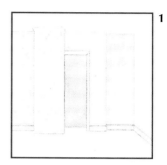

1 Paste the first length of paper you are going to hang around the doorway as if it were being hung on a plain section of wall.

2 Position it on the wall above the doorway in the normal way, allowing it to hang loosely over the frame.

3 Use a pair of long-bladed scissors to roughly cut the excess paper around the frame, leaving about 1in overlap all the way around.

4 At the corner, at the top of the frame, make a short diagonal cut in the overlap to allow the paper to lie flat.

5 Now brush the entire length of paper flat, pressing the overlap into the angle between the frame and the wall.

6 Carefully peel the overlapping paper back from the door frame and cut it off using your long-bladed scissors.

7 Repeat the process on the other side of the doorway.

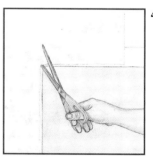

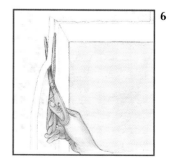

PAPERING AROUND A WINDOW

A flush window – one that does not jut out from the line of the house-wall – can be treated like a doorway. Simply hang the lengths of paper on the wall above the window and trim them to fit around the frame as described on page 33.

A recessed window needs to be treated in a slightly different way, but again there is no need to measure and pre-cut the wallcovering.

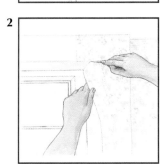

1 Paste the first length of paper that will overlap the window and position it on the wall above the opening. Let it loosely hang over the window soffit and reveal.

2 Press the paper against the edge of the soffit and cut along this line with a trimming knife, taking care not to tear the wallcovering.

3 This will allow you to wrap the paper below the cut around the angle of the wall and cover the reveal. Trim this paper where it overlaps the window frame.

4 Cut a small rectangle of wallcovering just large enough to overlap the reveal and soffit edges and fit this into the soffit-end.

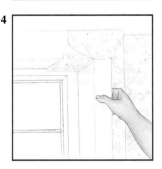

5 Brush the paper on the wall above, and to the side of this offcut, over the edges.

OPPOSITE: A flush window in a cottage room is pleasantly framed by contrasting wallcoverings and a coordinated border, giving a professional but atmospheric finish.

PAPERING AROUND A FIREPLACE

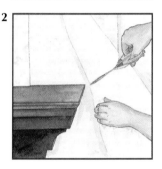

Paper around a fireplace in much the same way that you would around a window or door frame, positioning a full length of wallcovering on the chimney breast above the opening and allow this to loosely overhang the mantlepiece before attempting to make any cuts.

1 Lightly crease the wallcovering along the right-angled joint where the back of the mantlepiece butts up against the chimney breast.

2 Carefully peel the paper back from the mantlepiece and trim the waste paper below this crease with a pair of long-bladed scissors. Do not cut the full length of the crease at this stage – leave an inch overhanging the mantlepiece to allow for any slight adjustments when the paper is sitting completely flat against the wall on either side.

3 Press the paper at either side of the fireplace against the uprights that support the mantlepiece, again lightly creasing it to indicate where it should be cut.

4 Peel the paper away and trim the excess off to within an inch or two of these creases.

5 Use a pair of short-bladed scissors to finish off the trimming around any moldings or tight corners. Long-bladed scissors will give you a better edge along the back of the mantlepiece.

OPPOSITE: A traditional flock wallcovering adds grandeur and regency to the focal point of this room.

2

3

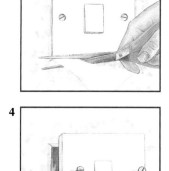

4

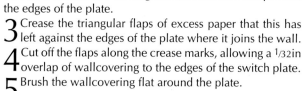

PAPERING AROUND A LIGHTSWITCH

You should always switch off the electricity supply at the mains before papering around a lightswitch. Different techniques are used for papering around either a square or a round switchplate.

Here is how to tackle a square plate:

1 Hang the length of wallcovering in the normal way, brushing it flat at the top and pressing it gently over the switch plate to mark its outline on the back of the paper. Do not brush it onto the wall below the switch at this stage.

2 Pierce the wallcovering somewhere near the center of the switchplate and then make four diagonal cuts outward from this point to the four corners of the plate. A pair of short-bladed scissors is ideal for this job.

3 Fold back the four triangular flaps of paper this has created so that you can see the whole of the face of the switch plate. Trim the flaps back so that they only overlap the sides of the plate by 1/8in or so.

4 Unscrew the plate and pull it about 1/4in away from the wall. Carefully pull the plate through the hole you have cut in the wallcovering, then press the paper behind the plate flat against the wall.

5 Tuck the flaps behind the plate and then brush the bottom half of the length into position. Then screw the switchplate back into place.

Here is how to tackle a circular switchplate:

1 Hang the length of paper in the normal way, brushing it into place along the top of the wall, and pressing it over the switch to mark its position on the back of the paper.

2 Pierce the wallcovering over the center of the switch, and make about 8-10 diagonal cuts out from this point to the edges of the plate.

3 Crease the triangular flaps of excess paper that this has left against the edges of the plate where it joins the wall.

4 Cut off the flaps along the crease marks, allowing a 1/32in overlap of wallcovering to the edges of the switch plate.

5 Brush the wallcovering flat around the plate.

OPPOSITE: The bold pattern and dark subtle colorings make this study an inviting and pleasurable workplace.

PAPERING BEHIND A RADIATOR

4

6
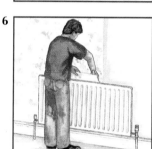

How much care you take to paper behind a radiator depends on how visible your handiwork will be.

It is physically impossible to look behind a radiator that has been fixed to the wall immediately below a window sill, so there is little point in papering the whole wall here.

It makes more sense to hang strips of wallcovering below the sill and above the baseboard, each finishing a couple of inches behind the radiator.

A radiator that is fixed to a plain wall will need to be tackled rather differently, as the whole of the wall area behind it will be visible to the inquiring eye.

But however visible the wall is, it is not necessary to remove a radiator from the wall in order to paper behind and around it, and few people do. It is perfectly possible to do the job with the radiator left in place if you know how.

1 Paste only the top half of any length of wallcovering that is going to hang down behind a radiator.

2 Position this on the wall and brush it flat in the normal way, with the bottom half hanging loosely over the top of the radiator.

3 Carefully feed the bottom edge of the paper down behind the radiator from above, pushing it down just far enough to crease it against the radiator bracket(s).

4 Pull the paper back up from behind the radiator and make a vertical cut up through the paper along the line initiated by this crease. This cut should run from the top of the baseboard to the top of the radiator bracket, where two small diagonal cuts need to be made to ease the paper around the bracket.

5 Fold the wallcovering gently back up the wall to paste the lower half, taking care not to make any splashes.

6 When the paste has soaked in, feed the paper back down behind the radiator, using a long-handled paint roller to press it flat against the wall.

Papering around a wall-mounted air-conditioning unit is a combination of the fireplace and the radiator techniques.

PAPERING AN ARCHWAY

Papering an archway between two rooms presents you with a similar problem to papering an external corner only worse – the wallcovering will crease horribly if you attempt to turn more than an inch or so around its edges.

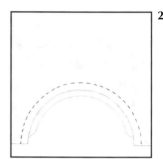

1 Hang each length of paper that will overlap the archway as normal, brushing it flat along its top edge but letting it hang down loosely over the opening.

2 Press it against the archway to mark the opening's outline on the reverse of the wallcovering, and then trim off the excess to within 1in of this mark.

3 Cut a series of triangles out of the remaining strip of excess wallcovering so that it will lie flat on the face of the arch. Paste the overlap onto the face of the arch. Repeat this process all the way around the arch.

4 Now measure the width of the face of the arch, and cut a strip of wallcovering long enough to cover it from the floor to its apex. Cut a longer strip if you have a pattern to match. Paste this length into position and then repeat the process, working from the other side of the archway.

NEXT PAGE: When wallpapering a ceiling pleasing effects can be achieved by mixing colors, textures, and patterns.

'Anaglypta', Crown Berger

Home Workshop
WORKING OVERHEAD

You have already learned many of the basic skills required to tackle ceilings in Section Two of this book, because a ceiling is papered in much the same way as a plain wall.

Do not be put off by the prospect of working at height – nor by visions of the paper drooping down around your ears at the moment that you turn your back. With a little planning, papering a ceiling can be a straightforward and satisfying job.

PREPARING THE ROOM

It is important that you cover the floor and any furniture that you cannot move out of the room with dustsheets. Filler, paste, and sticky offcuts of paper will all take their toll on an unprotected carpet.

It also makes sense to protect your eyes from flying debris when working overhead, so equip yourself with a pair of plastic goggles.

It is both safer and more convenient to stand on a work platform rather than a single ladder when you are papering ceilings. You can create your own working platform from two trestle tables or a pair of ladders with a scaffold-board hung between them. Arrange the platform so that you paper the full length of the ceiling in one go – if you can. You will probably need to use two boards, one placed on top of the other, if the distance between the platform ends is much more than 6ft.

If you do not have – or cannot borrow – any of this equipment, you can hire working platforms inexpensively from tool rental stores.

Arrange the platform so that you have just enough room to stand up straight on it without hitting your head on the ceiling.

PREPARING THE CEILING

Papering a ceiling is not going to disguise serious cracks, lumps, or bumps. If you want to cover up imperfections of this kind, you would be better off using a textured paint.

Ceiling papers will cover up hairline cracks if both a lining paper and a decorative top covering are used, but essentially they should only be considered for decorative reasons.

If the ceiling has been papered before, strip off the old covering, sand down any rough spots and smooth out all the cracks and hollows with filler.

Give the entire surface a coat of "size" (watered-down wallcovering paste) to reduce its absorbency. This will make it easier for you to slide lengths of paper across the ceiling if you need to adjust their position slightly once they have been hung.

WHERE TO START

Before you start, use a roll of paper as a measuring stick to work out on the carpet how many widths of paper you are going to have to hang. This exercise will indicate if you are going to be left with a very thin strip of paper to cut for the gap between the last full width of paper and the top of the far wall. If so trim 2in-4in off your first length to overcome this problem.

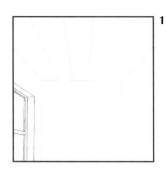

1 If the room only has windows along one wall, start papering immediately above this wall, hanging lengths parallel to it. This way, if there are any overlapping joints, they will not cast shadows on the ceiling.

2 If the room has windows on more than one wall, hang the paper across rather than along the ceiling. The shorter the lengths of paper you have to cope with, the easier the job will be.

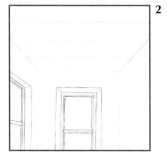

PAPERING THE CEILING

1

2

The joints between the walls and ceiling of the room you are decorating are unlikely to be perfectly smooth, so it makes sense to hang your first length of paper against a chalk mark and then trim it to fit.

1 Measure the width of your paper and then mark the ceiling this distance minus 1in from the top of the wall you are using as your starting point. Press a push-pin into the ceiling at this point and do the same at the far end of the room. Attach household string rubbed with chalk to these two pins and snap it against the ceiling to create your marking line.

2 Measure the length of the ceiling and add on 1in for an overlap at either end. Cut this much paper from your roll and paste it on a paste-table. Paste the entire length of paper in one go, folding it in to an accordion-style stack (paste-side to paste-side) as you go along. Make a fairly loose fold every 2ft, taking care not to crease the paper.

5

3 When the entire length has been pasted and the correct soaking time has elapsed, pick up the accordion style stack and climb onto one end of your work platform.

4 Unpeel the top edge of the paper and position it against your chalk mark, so that about 1in overlaps the end wall and a similar amount overlaps the side (window) wall.

5 Brush this first section of paper smooth against the ceiling before unpeeling the second fold and repeating the process. You may find that an extra pair of hands to hold the accordion style stack comes in useful here.

6 Align the second section of paper against your chalk mark and again brush it smooth before unpeeling any more paper. In this way, you should never have more than 2ft of paper to handle at any one time. The rest will either be in your hand, or firmly attached to the ceiling.

8

7 If the paper refuses to stick to the ceiling, you have probably made the paste too watery. Fold the paper back into an accordion style stack, mix some more and apply this to the ceiling. Then slide the paper back into place.

8 When you have hung the first length, trim its edges to fit the joints between the ceiling and the tops of the walls.

9 Hang the second and each successive length in exactly the same way, until you reach the far side of the room.

Photography props supplied by:

Nina Barough Styling

As credited, photographic material reproduced by kind permission of:

Forbo-Lancaster Limited
Storeys Decor
Crown Berger
Forbo-CP Limited